ROCKING RHYMES

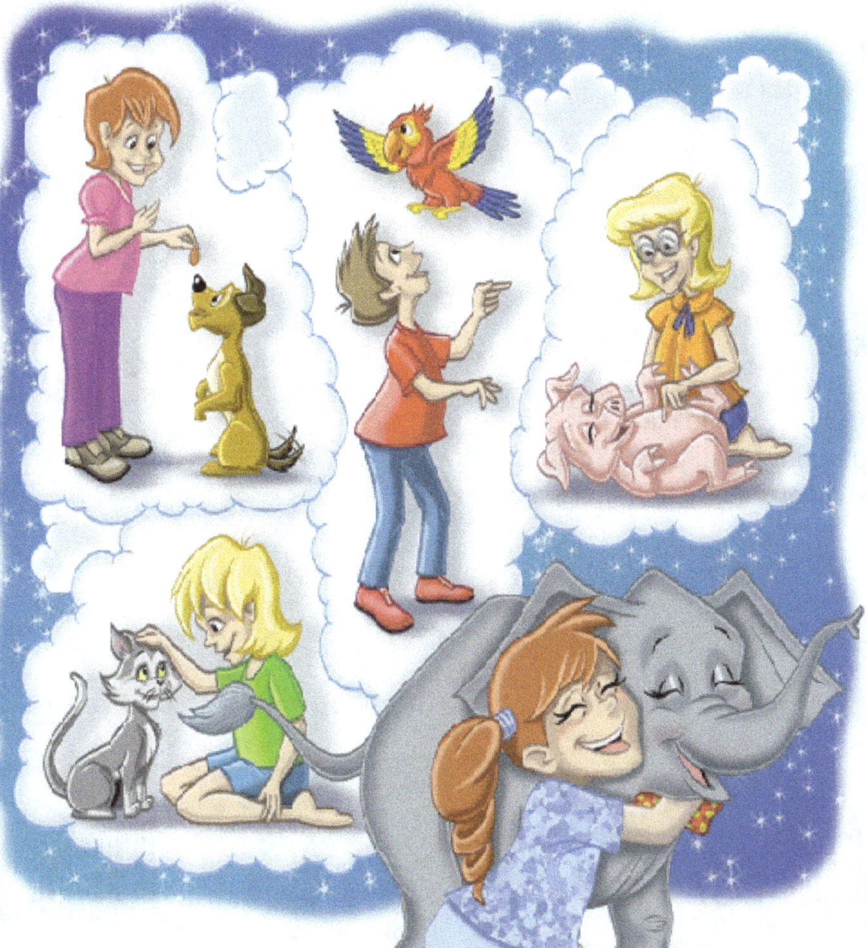

- RENU MATHUR

BOOKS-INDIA.COM
पुस्तक भारती
Since 1990

Pustak Bharati, Toronto, Canada

Author :
Renu Mathur

Book Title :
Rocking Rhymes

Published by :
PUSTAK BHARATI (Books India)
 Toronto, Ontario, Canada, M2R 3E4
 email : pustak.bharati.canada@gmail.com
 Web : www.pustak-bharati-canada.com

Copyright ©2022
ISBN 978-1-989416-54-9

ISBN 978-1-989416-54-9

© All rights reserved. No part of this book may be copied, reproduced or utilised in any manner or by any means, computerised, e-mail, scanning, photocopying or by recording in any information storage and retrieval system, without the permission in writing from the author.

INDEX

1.	Let Us Read And Sing	1
2.	Morning	2
3.	Sing A Song	3
4.	Doctor	4
5.	Fairy	5
6.	Ball	6
7.	Play Time	7
8.	Good Day	8
9.	Blue	9
10.	Johney Uncle	10
11.	Early Morning	11
12.	School	12
13.	Red Day	13
14.	Winters	14
15.	Moon	15
16.	School Bus	16
17.	Merry Christmas	17
18.	Days Of The Week	18
19.	A - B - C	19
20.	Purple - Day Game of Colours	20
21.	Rainbow	21
22.	God	22
23.	Tricycle	23
24.	Flowers	24
25.	Sky	25
26.	Rain	26
27.	Summer	27
28.	Our - Country	28
29.	Love Nature	29
30.	Miracles Of Touch	30
31.	My Sweet Lovely Daughter	31
32.	Aim	32

33.	Eyes	33
34.	Friendship	34
35.	Hope	35
36.	Leader	36
37.	Peace	37
38.	Tea	38
39.	Water	39
40.	Happy Birthday	40
41.	Relations	41
42.	Confusion In Life	42
43.	Red Day	43
44.	Truth Of Life	44
45.	Life Is Beautiful	45
46.	Our Sweet World	46
47.	Pray Teacher	47
48.	Teacher	48
49.	Why War	49
50.	Struggle	50
51.	Om	51
52.	Eyes	52
53.	Hands	53
54.	Human Body	54
55.	Dear Children	55
56.	Children	56
	About the Author	57

PREFACE

Children! The little readers, I am sure, you will enjoy reading and chanting the colourful poems of this book which has especially been written and designed for you. You can enjoy reading and learning while in bed or in the garden. You will come to know about various things you find around you in everyday life in a playful manner.

I want to thank Pustak Bharti Canada for accepting my book for publication.

I also thank people who helped me, Late Mr. Rajesh Mathur, Dr. Sunil Mathur, Mr. Anil Anwar, a well-known writer and all my family members.

Your well-wisher,
Renu Mathur

Let Us Read And Sing

MORNING

I WILL GET UP
FROM MY BED
BEFORE THE SUN GETS
GOLDEN RED

I WILL EAT
BUTTER AND BREAD
AND THEN WILL READ
A TO ZED

SING A SONG

**TRING TRING TRING
PHONES RING**

**SING SING SING
BIRDS SING**

**DRINK DRINK DRINK
SOFT DRINK**

DOCTOR

DOCTOR ! DOCTOR !
COME SOON

DOLLY IS SICK
SINCE NOON

GIVE HER A PILL
WITH A BOON

TO MAKE HER SMILE
LIKE MOON

FAIRY

SLEEPING SWEET FAIRY
UNDER A SHED
ON SOFT SILKY BED OF
ROSES RED

SHE IS LICKING HER
LIPS IN THE DREAM
LET HER FINISH
HER ICE - CREAM

BALL

IF YOU CLIMB
THE BOUNDRY WALL

YOU MIGHT HAVE
A GREAT FALL

RUN FAST CHILDREN
IT IS A TEACHER'S CALL

GO TO THE GARDEN
PLAY WITH THE BALL

PLAY TIME

COME TOGETHER
GIRLS AND BOYS

MAKE A QUEUE
WITHOUT ANY NOISE

TURN BY TURN
TAKE YOUR TOYS

PLAY WITH THEM
AND SHARE THE JOY

BLUE

IF I WERE THE SHINING STAR

I COULD REACH THE SKY BLUE

IF I WERE THE GOLDEN FISH

I COULD SWIM IN THE SEA BLUE

IF I WERE THE SWEET BIRD

I COULD FLY LIKE THE BIRD BLUE

JHONEY UNCLE

JHONEY UNCLE IS GOING
TO CATCH A TRAIN

HE HAS FASTENED
HIS BAG WITH CHAIN

IN HURRY TO REACH
THE STATION MAIN

FORGOT THE UMBRELLA
NOW WILL GET WET IN RAIN

EARLY MORNING

I GET-OFF MY BED
SO EARLY IN THE MORNING

I BRUSH MY TEETH
SO EARLY IN THE MORNING

I TAKE MY BATH
SO EARLY IN THE MORNING

I PRAY TO GOD
SO EARLY IN THE MORNING

I GO TO SCHOOL
SO EARLY IN THE MORNING

I READ AND WRITE
SO EARLY IN THE MORNING

I GO AROUND THE MANGO TREE
SO EARLY IN THE MORNING

SCHOOL

GOING TO SCHOOL
IS FUN

IN THE GARDEN
WE ALL RUN

DAUTHTERS OF INDIA
AND HER SONS

WE WILL RISE
BRIGHT LIKE SUN

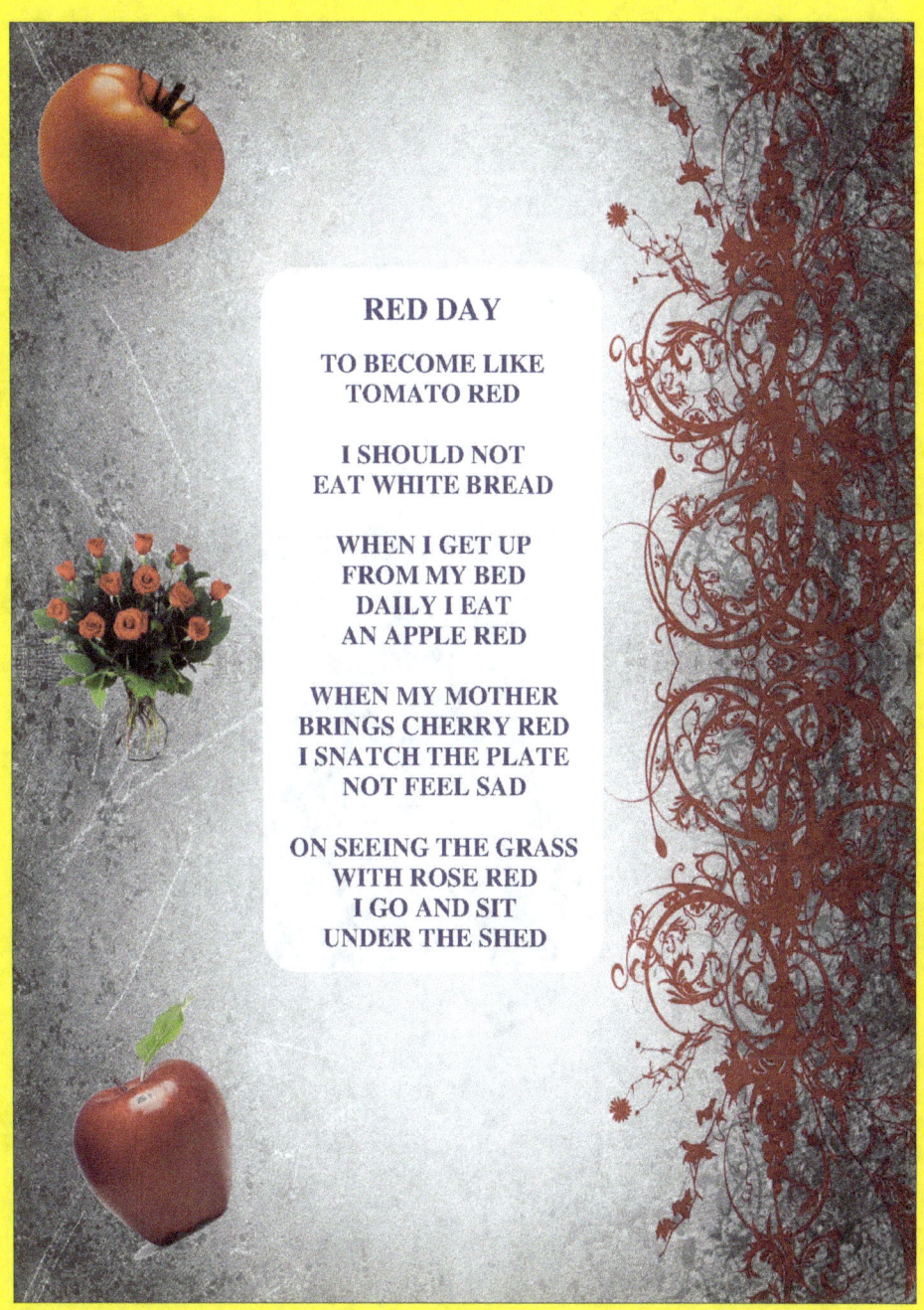

RED DAY

TO BECOME LIKE
TOMATO RED

I SHOULD NOT
EAT WHITE BREAD

WHEN I GET UP
FROM MY BED
DAILY I EAT
AN APPLE RED

WHEN MY MOTHER
BRINGS CHERRY RED
I SNATCH THE PLATE
NOT FEEL SAD

ON SEEING THE GRASS
WITH ROSE RED
I GO AND SIT
UNDER THE SHED

WINTERS

"O" SUN DEAR
WE CAN'T BEAR
WITHOUT YOU A SINGLE DAY

CAN'T YOU HEAR
COME CLOSE AND NEAR
TO WARM US ON A CHILLY DAY

IF YOU ARE HERE
I VOW YOU DEAR
WILL GO TO SCHOOL EVERY DAY

MOON

IN THE DARK AT NIGHT
SHINES BRIGHT,
THE SILVER MOON
LIKE A FAIRY FLIES
WITH A MAGIC BOON

IT DISAPEARS, THEN COMES
WITH A SILVER STREEK
LOOKS SOFT, SILKY
AND SLEEK

SOMETIMES IT SHINES LIKE A
SILVER BALL IN EVERY TWO WEEKS
MUMMY CALLS ME MOON AND
PINCH ON MY SOFT CHEEKS

SCHOOL BUS

LOOK AT THAT
YELLOW VEHICLE
ITS OUR SCHOOL BUS
RUN FAST RUN FAST
TO CATCH THE SCHOOL BUS

SO MANY CHILDREN
SO MANY WINDOWS
NEVER PEEP FROM
SCHOOL BUS
RUN FAST RUN FAST
TO CATCH THE SCHOOL BUS

MOVES WITH ONE STEERING
AND WHEELS FOUR
WITH DRIVER UNCLE
AND CONDUCTOR
WE NEVER FEEL BORE
RUN FAST RUN FAST
TO CATCH THE SCHOOL BUS

MERRY CHRISTMAS

SNOW IS FALLING NIGHT AND DAY
MONTH IS DECEMBER 25th DAY
SANTA CLAUS MUST BE ON THE WAY

WITH HEAVY BAGS FULL OF SWEETS
LETS EXCHANGE WITH HIM THE GREETS
BANG BANG SOUND OF BANDS BEATS

SINGING EVERYBODY WITH FULL OF JOY
DANCING JUMPING EVERY GIRL AND BOY
MERRY CHRISMAS - MERRY CHRISTMAS

ENJOY ! ENJOY ! ENJOY !

DAYS OF THE WEEK

WE LIKE MOST THE DAY SUNDAY
B'CAUSE ITS ALWAYS A HOLIDAY

IT IS FOLLOWED BY MONDAYS
FEEL LAZY AND CALL IT A BLUEDAY

WE MARCH ON EVERY TUESDAY
FOR IT IS CALLED A MARCH DAY

GO OUT TO PLAY ON EVERY WEDNESDAY
OUR TEACHER CALLS IT A PLAY DAY

WE ALL ARE SCARED OF EVERY THURSDAY
B'CAUSE PRINCIPAL MADE IT A CHECKING DAY

DOCTOR COMES FOR CHECK UP ON FRIDAYS
SO ALL CALL IT THE MEDICAL DAY

GO BACK HOME EARLY ON SATURDAYS
FOR ITS HALF-DAY AND IS CALLED THE FUNDAY

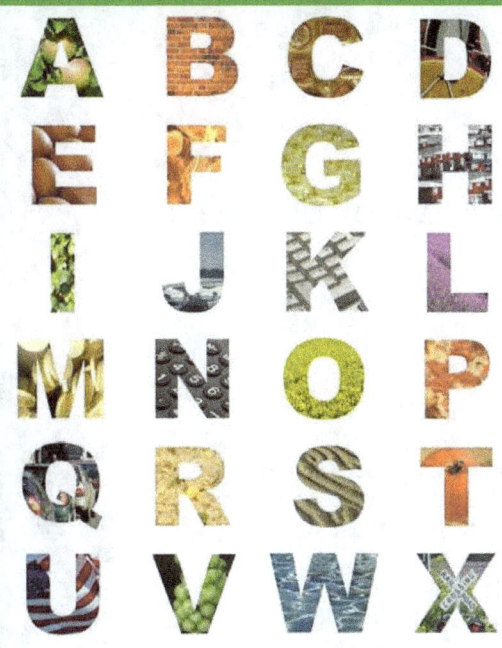

A - B - C

A B C D E
DRINK THE MILK AND NEVER TAKE TEA

F G H I J
TEACHER SHOW US THE RIGHT WAY

K L M N O
MAKE A NOISE ?
NO ! NO ! NO !

P Q R S T
ENJOY ENJOY IN THE PARTY

U V W X Y
SPEAK THE TRUTH NEVER TELL A LIE

Z, Z, Z, Z, Z
DON'T BE LAZY GET UP FROM YOUR BED

PURPLE - DAY GAME OF COLOURS

ITS A GAME, ITS A GAME
ITS A GAME OF COLOURS,
LET US PLAY THE GAME OF COLOURS.

CALL BLUE, CALL RED,
CALL PINK AND GREY,
CALL ORANGE, CALL WHITE,
CALL GREEN AND YELLOW
OH ! NO STILL MISSING
ONE COLOUR
WHICH IS THAT ?
CAN YOU NAME THAT COLOUR ?
ITS A GAME, ITS A GAME .....
LET .....

TO SOLVE THIS RIDDLE OF
COLOURS IN THE GAME
GIVING YOU THE HINT
WITH A FEW NAMES
IT IS FOUND IN THE VEGETABLE BRINJAL WE EAT
IT IS FOUND IN THE FRUIT BLACK BERRY WE EAT
ITS A GAME, ITS A GAME .....
LET US PLAY ....

YES, HERE COMES THE COLOUR PURPLE
NOW, HOLD THE HANDS AND MAKE A CIRCLE
ITS A GAME .....
LET US PLAY .....

RAINBOW

TO MAKE THE RAINBOW
WITH SEVEN COLOURS
LET US PLAY THE GAME OF COLOURS
ITS A GAME, ITS A GAME ITS A GAME OF COLOURS
LET US PLAY THE GAME OF COLOURS

CALL THE FRESH GRASS GREEN
PLAY ON IT AND KEEP IT CLEAN

CALL THE WIDE SKY BLUE
IT HAS SUN, MOON, STARS THAT GLUE

CALL THE MANGO WHICH IS YELLOW
IT IS LIKED BY EVERY FELLOW

CALL THE BEAUTIFUL ROSE RED
PRINCESS WALKS ON CARPET RED

CALL THE BRINJAL OF COLOUR VOILET
IT TURNS AROUND GET NEVER SET

CALL THE ORANGE FOR FRUIT JUICE
DRINK IT DAILY FOR HEALTHY USE

CALL THE BLACK BERRY WITH COLOUR INDIGO
GAME IS OVER LET GET, SET AND GO

NOW TO MAKE A SEMI-CIRCLE HOLD YOUR HANDS
COME ON CHILDREN CLAP YOUR HANDS

THIS IS HOW WE HAVE MADE THE RAINBOW
KEEP THE HEADS DOWN AND BOW.

ITS A GAME, ITS A GAME .....
LET US PLAY THE .....

TRICYCLE

TRIN TRIN TRIN
TRIN TRIN TRIN

I DRIVE MY TRICYCLE WITH THRILL
WHICH HAS HANDLE, SEATS AND THREE WHEELS
TRIN TRIN TRIN
TRIN TRIN TRIN

HOW SHINING IS ITS COLOUR RED
ON HADLE FLIES THE INDIAN FLAG
TRIN TRIN TRIN
TRIN TRIN TRIN

ON ITS BACK SEAT MY DEAR DAD
KEEPS MY HEAVY SCHOOL BIG BAG
TRIN TRIN TRIN
TRIN TRIN TRIN

I CARRY FLOWERS IN ITS BASKET
BRING FRUITS FROM THE FRUIT MARKET
TRIN TRIN TRIN
TRIN TRIN TRIN

IT RUNS FAST FAST AND FAST
AFRAID ITS TYRES SHOULD NOT BLAST
TRIN TRIN TRIN
TRIN TRIN TRIN

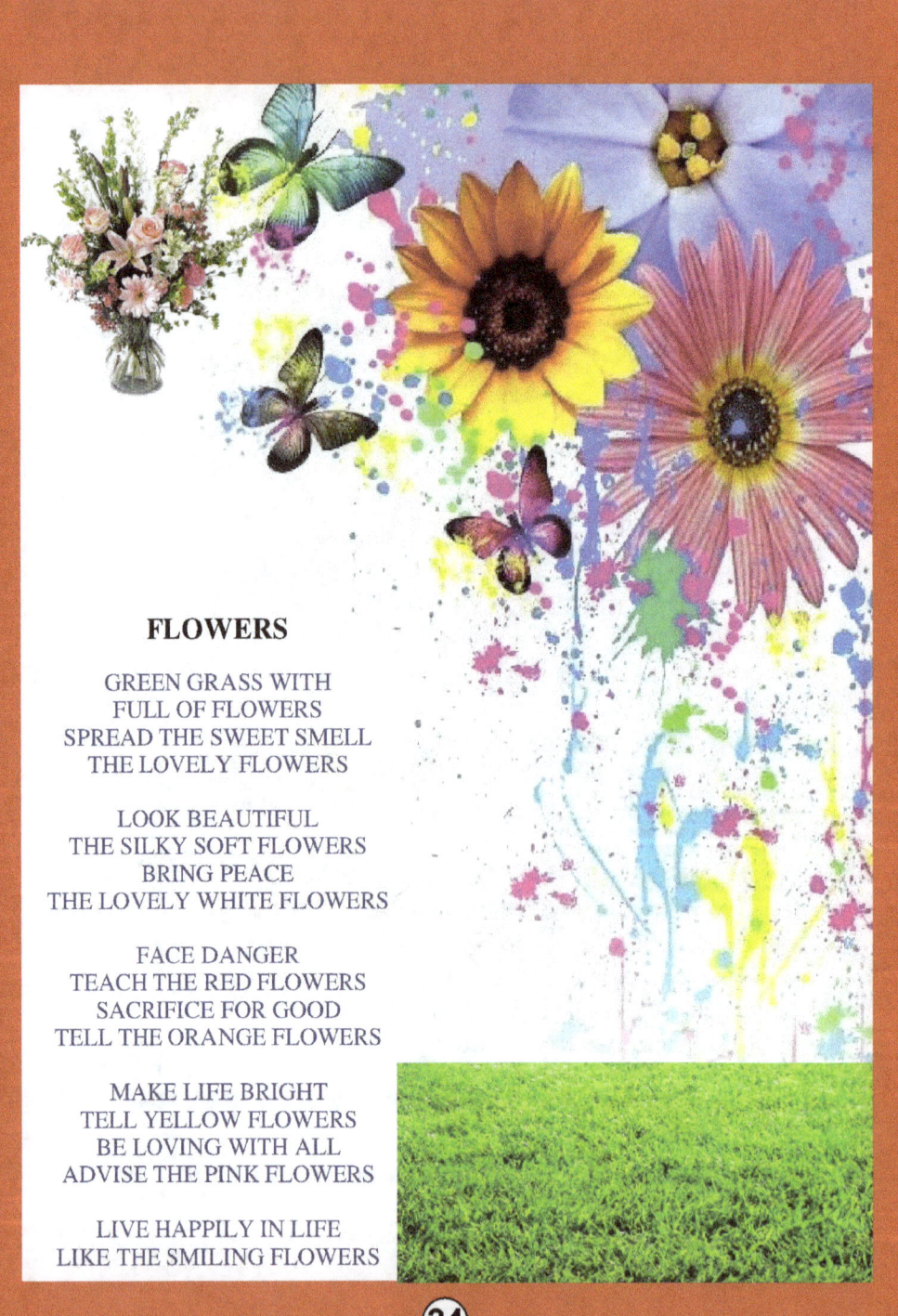

FLOWERS

GREEN GRASS WITH
FULL OF FLOWERS
SPREAD THE SWEET SMELL
THE LOVELY FLOWERS

LOOK BEAUTIFUL
THE SILKY SOFT FLOWERS
BRING PEACE
THE LOVELY WHITE FLOWERS

FACE DANGER
TEACH THE RED FLOWERS
SACRIFICE FOR GOOD
TELL THE ORANGE FLOWERS

MAKE LIFE BRIGHT
TELL YELLOW FLOWERS
BE LOVING WITH ALL
ADVISE THE PINK FLOWERS

LIVE HAPPILY IN LIFE
LIKE THE SMILING FLOWERS

SKY

BLUE IS THE COLOUR OF THE SKY
UMBRELLA LIKE SHELTER IS THE SKY
SUN THROWS RAYS FROM THE SKY
DAY ALLOWS BIRDS FLY IN THE SKY
MOON BRINGS PEACE IN THE SKY
NIGHT BRINGS DARKNESS IN THE SKY
SHINING STARS TWINKLE IN THE SKY
CLOUDS ROAM ALL AROUND IN THE SKY
RAINBOW IS A MIRACLE IN THE SKY
COLOURS SPREAD ALL OVER THE SKY
AEROPLANE TAKES US TO TOUCH THE SKY

RAIN

RAIN RAIN COME AGAIN
TO BRING FRESHNESS IN THE BRAIN

RAIN RAIN COME AGAIN
GIVE LIFE TO DEAD LEAVES AGAIN

RAIN RAIN COME AGAIN
TO MAKE PEASANTS GROW THE GRAIN

RAIN RAIN COME AGAIN
I ENJOY YOU WHEN IN TRAIN

SUMMER

O SUN GO AWAY
ITS SO HOT ALL THE DAY

I CAN'T EAT I CAN'T SLEEP
LIKE TO SWIM IN THE WATER DEEP
O SUN GO ....

KEEP SITTING IN THE ROOM MAIN
HAVE TO PLAY THE INDOOR GAME
O ! SUN GO ....

ITS SO HOT...............

OUR - COUNTRY

BANG BANG BEAT THE BAND
SING INDIA IS MY MOTHER LAND

THE WORLD LIKES INDIA THE MOST
WE ARE CALLED THE BEST HOST
BANG BANG .... SING ....

KASHMIR VALLEY IS OUR CROWN
ON EARTH HEAVEN IS BROUGHT DOWN
BANG BANG .... SING ....

HIMALAYA'S PEAKS ARE VERY HIGH
IT MAKES US THINK AND DREAM HIGH
BANG BANG .... SING ....

HOLIEST OF ALL IS GANGA RIVER
ITS COLD WATER MAKES US SHIVER
BANG BANG .... SING ....

MOSQUE, GURUDWARA TEMPLES ARE
INDIA'S BEAUTY
TO RESPECT THEM ALL IS OUR DUTY
BANG BANG .... SING ....

WE SPEAK HUNDREDS OF LANGUAGES
STILL ARE UNITED SINCE THE AGES
BANG BANG .... SING ....

OUR TRICOLOUR FLAG IS VERY SMART
UNDER IT STAND THE DIFFERENT CASTS
BANG BANG .... SING ....

GOD HAS CREATED THIS SPLENDID NATURE,
FULL OF DIFFERENT KINDS OF CREATURES.
THE UNIVERSE IS FULL OF WONDERS,
ONE LIFE IS LESS TO ENJOY THE WONDERS.
LIVING, NON-LIVING THINGS ARE THERE,
WHICH BEAUTIFY THE WORLD EVERYWHERE.
FRESH WINDS AND RIVERS KEEP ON FLOWING.
NOBODY KNOWS FROM WHERE THEY KEEP COMING
AND WHERE THEY KEEP GOING.
FLOWERS, BIRDS, ANIMALS ADD BEAUTY SCENCES
MOON AND STARS GLITTER WITH THEIR BEAMS.
SUN RISES TO BRING A NEW DAY IN LIFE,
GOOD SPIRIT SPREADS IN EVERYBODY'S LIFE.
WE MUST SAVE, PROTECT AND LOVE OUR NATURE,
FOR GENERATIONS TO COME IN THE NEAR FUTURE.

RENU MATHUR

MIRACLES OF TOUCH

MIRACLE IS THE SENSE OF FEELINGS,
A MAGIC FOR WOUNDS OF HEART HEALING.
TOUCH AND FEEL IS THE LIFE'S GAME
WHEN BOTH SIDES THINK THE SAME
ONE EATS WHEN ONE FEELS HUNGRY,
ONE SHOUTS WHEN ONE FEELS ANGRY
IT IS WONDERFUL TO BE IN LOVE
WITH PARENTS, CHILDREN OR BELOVED
========

RENU MATHUR

ॐ

O' MY SWEET,
LOVELY
DAUGHTER
YOU ARE AS
PRECIOUS AS
WATER

BE KIND,
HONEST N
COURAGEOUS
LIFE IS
STRUGGLEFUL N
TEDIOUS

BY GRACE OF
GOD YOU ARE
WISE
WORK HARD FOR
GOAL IS ADVICE

*****ALL THE
VERY BEST*****

RM 9649473939

WITH PARENTS, CHILDREN OR BELOVED

========   RENU MATHUR

31
30

AIM

MAKE YOUR AIM INLIFE
TO ACHIEVE HEIGHTS IN LIFE
CONFUSION ARISES WITHOUT AIM IN LIFE
AIM IS THE POINT TO CONCENTRATE IN LIFE
HURDLES ARISE WITH OUR AIM IN LIFE
BUT BE FIRM TO STICK TO YOUR AIM
FOLLOW PATH OF TRUTH TO GET SUCCESS IN LIFE
YOU WILL BE HAPPY, WEALTHY AND WISE IN LIFE
GO AHEAD TO START A NEW BEGINNING IN LIFE.
ALL THE VERY BEST

RENU MATHUR

EYES

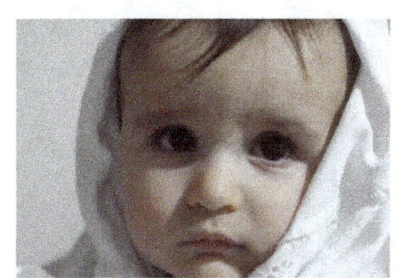

GOD HAS GIVEN US THE PRECIOUS EYES,
BEAUTIFUL WORLD CAN BE SEEN WITH EYES.
WE ENJOY GREENERY, FLOWERS, SCENERIES,
HILLS, STARS, MOON AND SUN WITH EYES.
COLOURED BIRDS CAN BE SEEN WITH EYES.
SMALLEST INSECT AND HUGE ANIMALS ALSO
CAN BE SEEN ONLY WITH THESE TWO EYES.
RIVERS, FALLS, SEA, CLOUDS AND RAIN,
CAN BE SEEN WITH THESE TWO EYES.
DIFF. KIND OF PEOPLE, FASHION AND STYLES,
CAN BE FULLY ENJOYED BY THESE TWO EYES.
TO KEEP OUR EYES BRIGHT AND SAFE
IS OUR DUTY TO TAKE CARE OF OUR BOTH EYES.

RENU MATHUR

FRIENDSHIP

TO GO ACROSS THE HUGE SEA.
WE BORROW A BOAT OR SHIP.
TO GET OVER THE STRESS OF LIFE,
ALL WE NEED IS **FRIENDSHIP**.

RENU MATHUR

HOPE

IN DEPRESSION ONE SHOULD NOT FEAR
ONE NEVER BRINGS IN EYES THE TEARS.

WHEN AT TIMES, YOU LOOSE HEART
SUN IS THERE TO GIVE YOU A NEW START

BE ALWAYS AWAKEN AND BRAVE
COURAGE COMES FROM THE SOUL GREAT

LET HOW DEEP THE BAD TIME BE
BRIGHT LIGHT SHALL COME YOU SEE

NIGHTS ARE SOMETIMES EXTREMELY DARK
BUT SUN RAYS CAN GO THROUGH DARKEST DARK

NO HARM PUTTING LIFE ON TEST
LET US 'HOPE'   FOR THE BEST

RENU MATHUR

LEADER

A LEADER IS ONE WHO TAKES THE FIRST STEP,

A LEADER IS ONE WHO TEACHES EACH AND EVERY STEP.

A LEADER IS ONE WHO IS HONEST IN EVERY FIELD

A LEADER IS ONE WHO NEVER RUNS AWAY FROM BATTLE FIELD.

A LEADER IS ONE WHO IS FEARLESS AND VIGILENT,

A LEADER IS ONE WHO IS WISE AND INTELLIGENT.

A LEADER IS ONE WHO CAN FORESEE THE SITUATION,

A LEADER IS ONE WHO CHANGES TEAM'S POSITION.

A LEADER IS ONE WHO BELIEVES IN VICTORY,

A LEADER IS ONE WHO CREATES A HISTORY.

RENU MATHUR

PEACE

WE ALL WISH TO BE IN PEACE

TO BELIEVE IN TRUTH IS PEACE

TO SERVE MANKIND IS PEACE

TO BE POSITIVE IS PEACE

GOOD DEEDS GIVE PEACE

KEEP SMILING IS PEACE

TO REMAIN HAPPY IS PEACE

TO BE HONEST IS PEACE

TO HAVE FAITH IN GOD GIVES PEACE

RENU MATHUR

TEA

ITS NOT MODERN BUT ANANCIENT BELIEF,

MAKES EVERYONE HAPPY OR IN GRIEF.
NATURE HAS GIFTED US THE TEA LEAF,
THAT GIVES MILLIONS THE ENTIRE RELIEF.
ASIA, US, EUROPE OR GREES,
ITS POPULAR IN EVERY STREET.
ONE FEELS SLEEPY OR WEAK,
TAKES A SIP AND FEEL SLEEK.
TO GET-OFF BED IT HELPS AND GREET,
INDEEDTEA IS LIFE ONE CAN SAY IN BRIEF.

RENU MATHUR

WATER

ALL WE UNDERSTAND THE VALUE OF GOLD.
IT MAKES WEALTHY WHETHER NEW OF OLD,
TO PROTECT AND SAVE THE GOLD WITH CARE,
TO POSSESS, KILLING FIGHTING NOT FAIR,
GOLD CAN ONLY MAKES HIGH STATUS IN LIFE
WATER IS PROVED TO BE THE ELIXIR OF LIFE
WITHOUT GOLD NO ONE DIES,
WITHOUT WATER THERE IS NO LIFE,

WATER IS PRECIOUS DON'T WASTE THE SAME

NEVER GROW OLD
REMAIN IN YOUR TEEN
RARE PEOPLE ARE ALWAYS EVERGREEN

ITS GOD'S BLESSINGS I AM SURE AND MEAN
REMAIN ALWAYS SAFE HEALTHY AND CLEAN

RELATIONS

ITS TO FEEL FOR ONE-ANOTHER
TO DO ALL THINGS ALWAYS TOGETHER.

TO MAKE LIFE POSSIBLE ON THE EARTH,
SUN SHINES AND EVERYDAY TAKES BIRTH.

TO KEEP RELATIONS WITH THE SUN,
EARTH MOVES DAILY AROUND THE SUN.

RIVERS FLOWS ALL DAY AND NIGHT,
TO MERGE IN THE SEA, THEIR KNIGHT.

GOD IS THE FATHER OF ALL,
LOOKS AFTER THEM EVEN IN THEIR FALL
RENU MATHUR

CONFUSION IN LIFE

SINCE THE DAY I WAS BORN LIKE ALL,
AM LEARNING EACH AND EVERYTHING.
TILL DATE I FIND DIFFCULT TO FIND,
BETWEEN GOOD AND A BAD THING.

WHEN I DOUBT ANYBODY,
I DO NOT TELL HIM ANYTHING.
WHEN I TRUST ANYBODY,
I REPENT WHY TOLD EVERYTHING.

WHEN I PUNISH ANYBODY,
CURSE MYSELF HAS DONE A SILLYTHING.
WHEN I WANT TO BE A REAL HUMAN BEING,
CAN'T FORGIVE AND FORGET ANYTHING.

RENU MATHUR

RED DAY

TO BECOME LIKE TOMOATO RED
  WE SHOOULD NOT EAT WHITE BREAD
  WHEN WE GET UP FROM MY BED
  DAILY WE EAT APPLES RED
WHEN OUR MOTHERS BRING CHERRY RED
  WE SNATCH THE PLATE AND FEEL GLAD
ON SEEING THE GRASS WITH ROSES RED
WE GO AND SIT UNDER THE TREES SHED

RENU MATHURE

TRUTH OF LIFE

YOU MAY HAVE PLENTY OF WEALTH AND A LUXURIOUS LIFE
THESE THINGS ARE USELESS IF YOU ARE NOT WISE
TALENT, NAME AND FAME ARE IMPORTANT FOR YOU,
THESE CAN'T TELL WHAT IS GOOD AND BAD FOR YOU.
IF YOU REALLY WANT TO BE A GENTLEMAN,
THEN FOLLOW THE PATH OF THE GREATMEN.
NEWTON AND SWAMI VIVEKANANDA ARE THE EXAMPLE,
EARNED FAME AND NAME THROUGH WISDOM AND PRINCIPLE
SERVE POOR, NEEDY AND DO GOOD DEEDS,
IT WILL REAP YOU GOOD FRUITS AND SEEDS

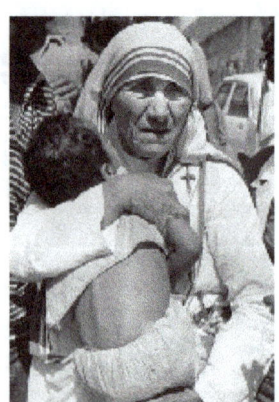

RENU MATHUR

LIFE IS BEAUTIFUL LET US SHARE,
SORROWS AND JOYS EVERYWHERE.
ENJOY NATURE, FRESH AIR, FLOWERS AND SCENERY,
WITH FALLS, RAINS, SNOW, CLOUDS AND GREENERY,
TO MAKE IT MORE WONDERFUL DAY BY DAY,
LET US HELP THE POOR AND NEEDY EVERYDAY.
NO ONE SHOULD BE LEFT ALONE,
LET US SING IN ONE TONE

"WORLD IS MIRACLE AND ABOON OF GIFT
WHICH MAKES US HAPPY, HEALTY AND FIT"

OUR SWEET WORLD

GOD HAS CREATED THIS WORLD SO BEAUTIFUL,
HAS ALSO MADE THE LIVING BEINGS CHEERFUL.
BEAUTIFUL GREENERY AND BEAUTIFUL COLOURED BIRDS,
THEIR CHIRPING EXPRESS HAPPY AND SORROWS WORDS.
SONGS OF NIGHTINGALE PLAY AN IMPORTANT ROLE,
WHEN PEACOCKS DANCE, WE DANCE WITH OUR SOULS.
GIFT OF ANIMALS IS OF A TREMENDOUS HELP,
BECAUSE MANY A TASKS WE CAN'T DO SELF.
CAMELS ARE CALLED THE SHIPS OF DESERT,
COWS MILK HELP IN MAKING SWEET DESSERT.
DOGS ARE THE BEST FAITHFUL FRIEND,
WHERAS SNAKES BITE BRINGS LIFE TO AN END.

RENU MATHUR

PRAY TEACHER

I WORSHIP MY TEACHER,
BEFORE I PRAY TO GOD.
AND DON'T MIND HER SCOLDS
OR BEATS WITH RODS.

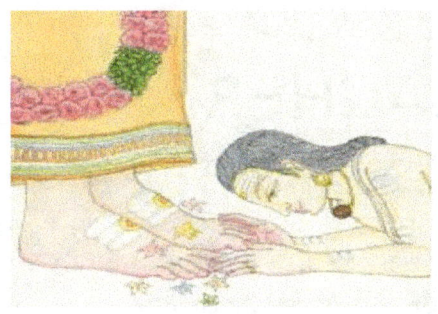

BECAUSE SHE WILL, I KNOW,
MAKE ME WISE AND BROAD.
FOR EACH AND EVERY DECISION,
I SEEK HER ADVICE AND NOD.

RENU MATHUR

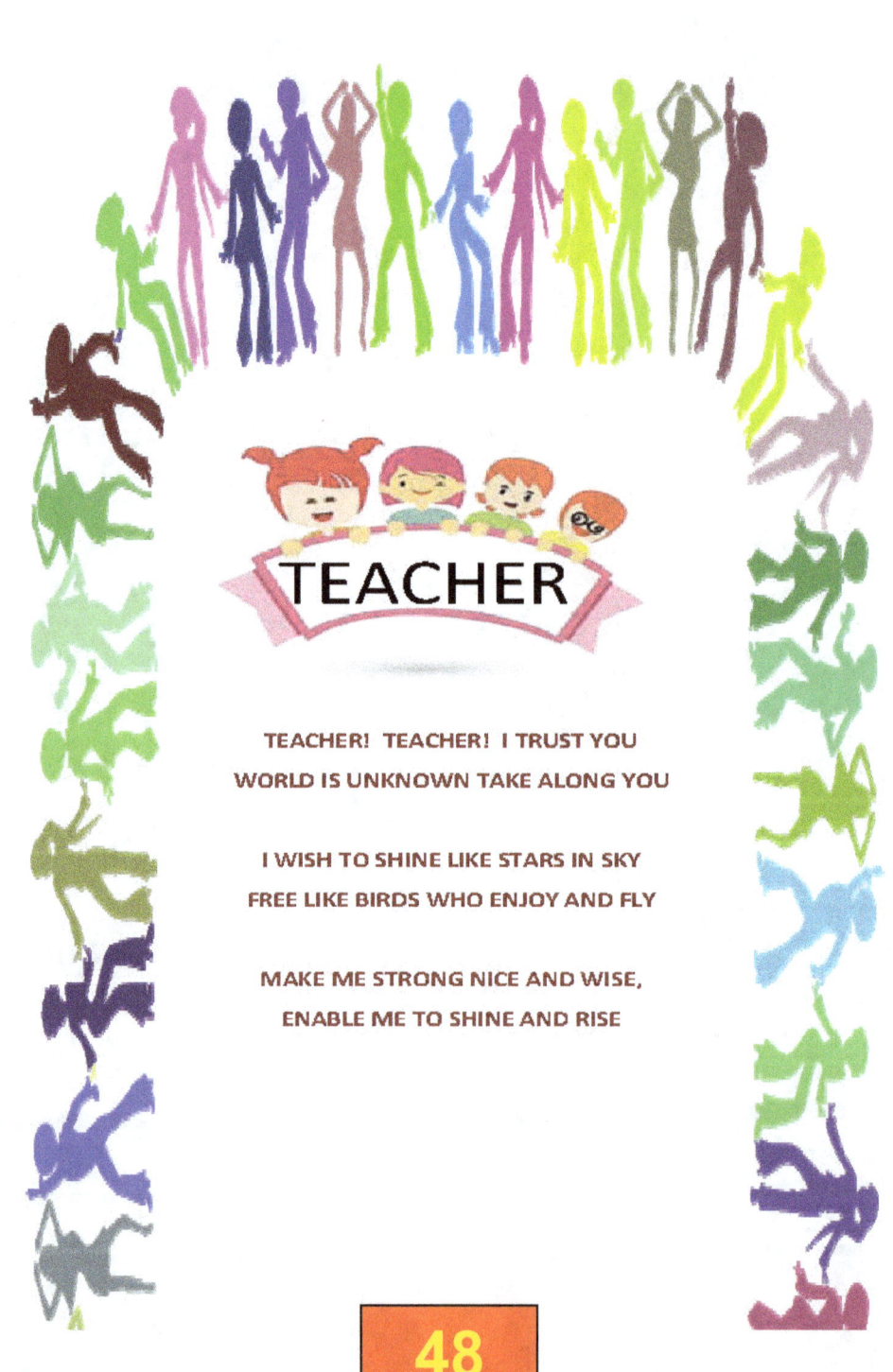

TEACHER

TEACHER! TEACHER! I TRUST YOU
WORLD IS UNKNOWN TAKE ALONG YOU

I WISH TO SHINE LIKE STARS IN SKY
FREE LIKE BIRDS WHO ENJOY AND FLY

MAKE ME STRONG NICE AND WISE,
ENABLE ME TO SHINE AND RISE

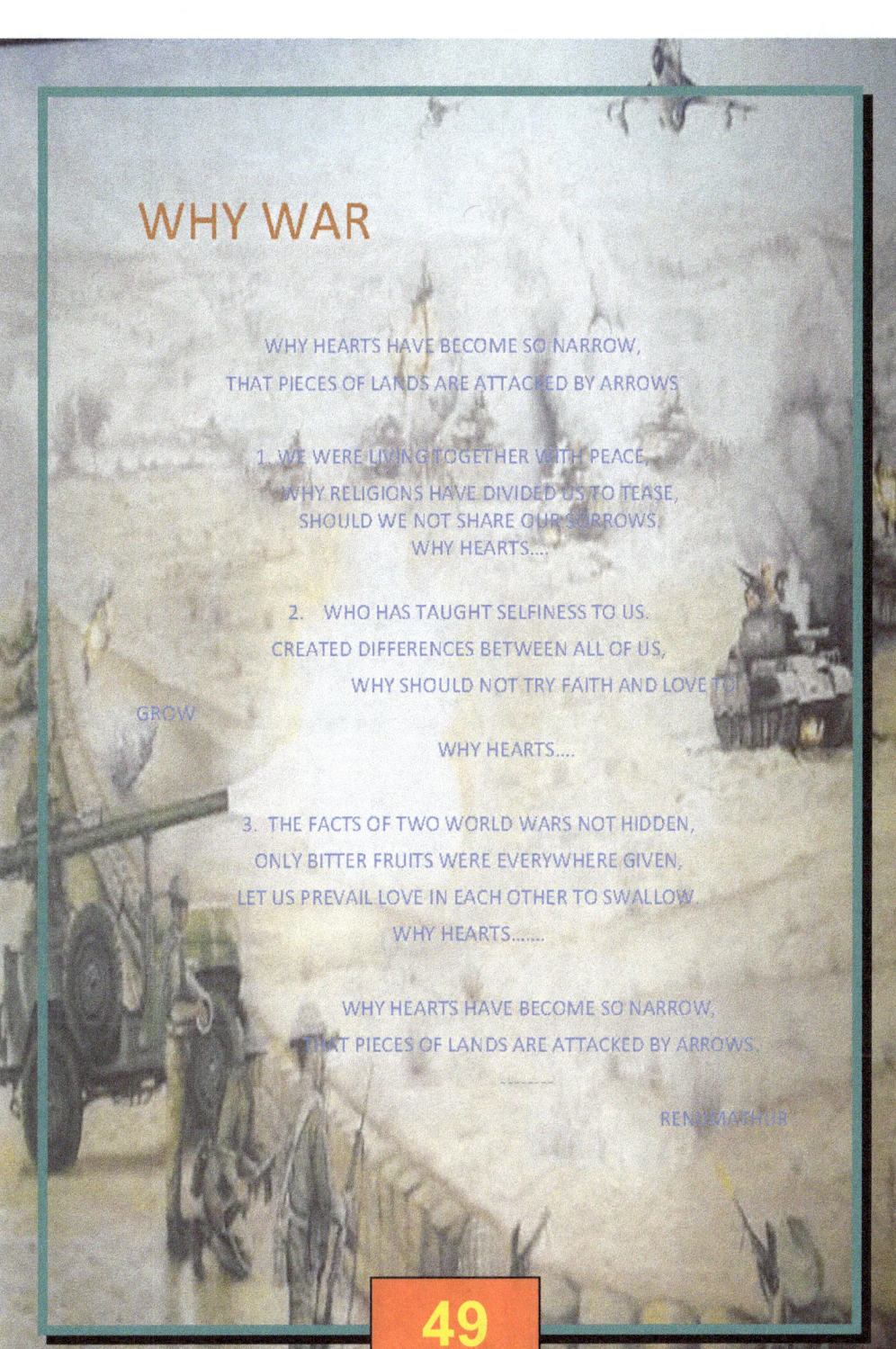

WHY WAR

WHY HEARTS HAVE BECOME SO NARROW,
THAT PIECES OF LANDS ARE ATTACKED BY ARROWS

1. WE WERE LIVING TOGETHER WITH PEACE,
WHY RELIGIONS HAVE DIVIDED US TO TEASE,
SHOULD WE NOT SHARE OUR SORROWS,
WHY HEARTS....

2. WHO HAS TAUGHT SELFINESS TO US,
CREATED DIFFERENCES BETWEEN ALL OF US,
WHY SHOULD NOT TRY FAITH AND LOVE TO GROW
WHY HEARTS....

3. THE FACTS OF TWO WORLD WARS NOT HIDDEN,
ONLY BITTER FRUITS WERE EVERYWHERE GIVEN,
LET US PREVAIL LOVE IN EACH OTHER TO SWALLOW,
WHY HEARTS.......

WHY HEARTS HAVE BECOME SO NARROW,
THAT PIECES OF LANDS ARE ATTACKED BY ARROWS.

RENU MATHUR

STRUGGLE

LIFE IS LIKE A COIN WITH TWO SIDES
ONE IS GOOD , BAD IS ON THE OTHER SIDE

WITHOUT THE TWO, LIFE IS OF NO USE
GOOD IS FELT WHEN STRUGGLE DEFUSED

FEEL HAPPY TO SPEND GOOD TIME
STRUGGLE ALSO THRILLS AT TIMES

RENU MATHUR

ॐ

WHEN A CHILD TAKES BIRTH
HE IS ALL ALONE ON THE EARTH

LAP HE GETS OF MOTHER FATHER
BASE OF LIFE IS THESE PREACHER

WORDLY LIFE TAUGHT BY TEACHER
RIGHT OR WRONG MAKE FUTURE

FOLLOW PATH SHOWN BY TEACHER
SUCCESS WILL BE SURE IN VENTURE

HAPPY TEACHERS DAY
****

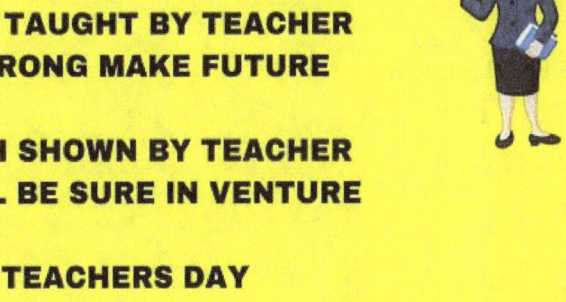

EYES

GOD HAS GIFTED US WITH PRECIOUS TWO EYES
BEAUTIFUL WORLD CAN BE SEEN WITH EYES

GREENERY, FLOWERS, HILLS, STARS AND SUN
HOW COLOURFUL BIRDS CHEER AND MAKE FUN

THE SMALLEST INSECT AND HUGE ANIMALS
EYES ESCAPE US FROM DANGEROUS MAMMALS

SUN, STARS, SKY, CLOUDS, FARMS AND GRAIN
EYES SHOW US RIVERS, SNOW AND RAIN

WE CAN DIFFERENTIATE BETWEEN BIG AND SMALL
WITH THE HELP OF THE TWO CUTE CUTE EYES

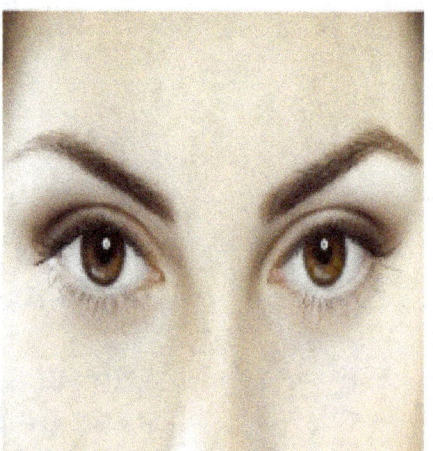

RENU MATHUR

HANDS

WE ARE BORN WITH TWO HANDS
WITH FIVE FINGERS IN EACH HAND
THE SMALL AND PYGMY IS THE THUMB
CAN'T WORK IF IT DOES NOT JUMP

NEXT COMES THE INDEX FINGER
HELPS SHOWING PATH TO STRANGER

THEN STANDS THE MIDDLE FINGER
THE TALLEST AMONG ALL FINGERS

THE MOST IMPORTANT IS THE RING FINGER
IT IS ALSO CALLED THE HEART FINGER

DEAREST IS THE SWEET LITTLE FINGER
YOUNGEST IN ALL THE FIVE FINGERS

PALM IS THEIR PLACE TO GO FOR SLEEP
MAKING A STRONG PUNCH WE BELIEVE

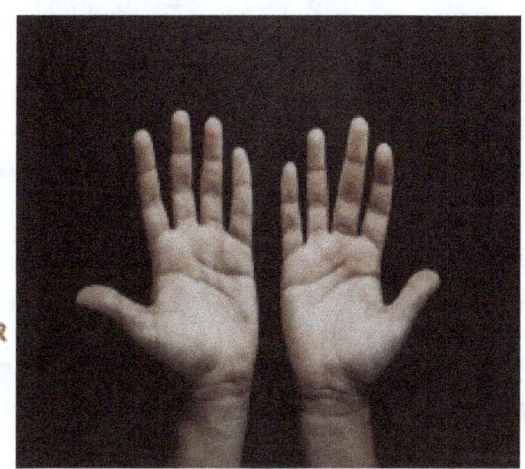

RENU MATHUR

HUMAN BODY

WE ARE LUCKY TO HAVE THIS MIRACLE BODY
AND ARE THANKFUL TO GOD FOR GIFT OF BODY

WE USE OUR BRAIN FOR EACH AND EVERYTHING
WITH THE HELP OF EYES CAN SEE EVERYTHING

WITH EARS WE LISTEN AND ENJOY THE NATURE SOUND
NOSE HELPS BREATHING AND SMELL THINGS AROUND

HEART AND VEINS HELP US CIRCULATE THE BLOOD
BELLY WORKS TO DIGEST THE SOFT AND HARD FOOD

TWO HANDS, ARMS HELP US WORK HARD TO DO
LEGS AND FEET TAKE US WHERE WE WISH TO GO

RENU MATHUR

Dear Children

O' My children come around
let us go to the playground
hold the hands of each other
make a circle and run around

We are called the human beings
trees, plants are living beings
we depend upon each other
for the welfare of each being

Smell of savory flowers
gives peace to our heart N soul
makes our minds to feel fresh
to work hard and achieve any goal

Soft and cool grass looks
like a natural carpet green
dew drops shining with colours
how glitters in Sun are seen

Renu Mathur

OM

CHILDREN
=========

WE CAN SEE THE SKY WITH
FULL OF GLITTERING STARS
FOR US OUR CHILDREN ARE
THE UPCOMING SHINING STARS

YOU LOOK LIKE FLOWERS IN
OUR GARDEN OF LIFE
YOUR FACES BLOSSOM AND
MAKE US FEEL FRESH IN LIFE

YOUR AROMA SPREADS AND
ACCENT IS SWEET CUTIE PIE
SOFT TOUCH PROMPT US ENJOY
EVERY MOMENT TO SURVIVE

RENU MATHUR

Renu Mathur

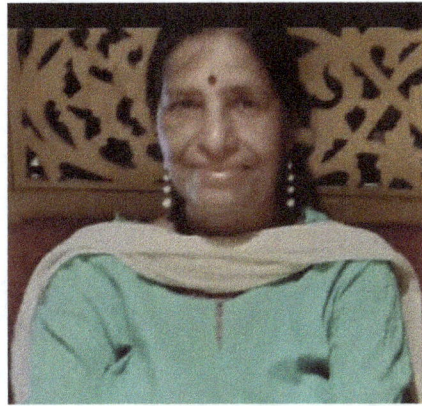

111A, Mansarovar, Pal Road Bypass,
Jodhpur-342001, Rajasthan, India

Mobile : +91 9649473939
Email : renumathur8@gmail.com

Education: Graduate in Arts from Delhi University
Profession: Retired as an Officer(Opted for VRS , from Customer Oriented Departments of the Main Branch of Standard Chartered Bank, New Delhi..

Publication: Poems, Articles in both the languages Hindi and English
Published namely in Maru-Gulshan Rajasthan, Daily News Rajasthan Patrika, Nari Asmita, Adhyatma Yoga Patrika, Vivekananda Sanstha magazine.
Ram-Gatha a poem based on Ramayana in just 40 lines describing each character's role from Balmiki to Luv-Kush
Similarly, a poem **Maha-Kavya** based on Mahabharta in just about 120 lines describing all the periods and characters of the epic, is under publication,
A book of collection for children's poems and songs in Hindi published by title
'AAO BACHCHON GAO GEET'
Book of Poems in English "**ROCKING RHYMES'** educating children about their surroundings with a difference while reading and playing.

National & International Awards

A certificate for poem - PARIVAR organized by Sahitya News awarded with the International Creation Award certificate 2020.

A certificate and a trophy for participation in the compiled book of poems in GOLDEN BOOK OF WORLD RECORDS - ARUN AWARDEES 'an international book

Commendable citation for Golden Book of World Records by Sports Authority of India.
Commendable certificate on Unique Contribution for Writing on Arjuna Awards by International Human Rights Organization.

A certificate for poem - PARIVAR organized by Sahitya News awarded with the International Creation Award 2020 certificate titled.

Commendable certificate for writing an article on 'Bharat Ratan Award', on Mother Terresa, the highest and the most precious award given in India, for outstanding work done by a citizen of India.

Certificate and a trophy for getting 2nd position for online poetryrecitation with title **ISTRI**(Lady) on **YouTube'Navratri Competition 2021'**.

www.ingramcontent.com/pod-product-compliance
Lightning Source LLC
Chambersburg PA
CBHW081312070526
44578CB00006B/846